Soluble Fish

Crab Orchard Series in Poetry

FIRST BOOK AWARD

Soluble Fish

MARY JO FIRTH GILLETT

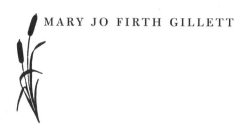

Crab Orchard Review

&

Southern Illinois University Press

CARBONDALE

10   09   08   07   4   3   2   1

The Crab Orchard Series in Poetry is a joint publishing venture of Southern Illinois
University Press and *Crab Orchard Review*. This series has been made possible by the
generous support of the Office of the President of Southern Illinois University and
the Office of the Vice Chancellor for Academic Affairs and Provost at Southern
Illinois University Carbondale.

Crab Orchard Series in Poetry Editor: Jon Tribble
First Book Award Judge for 2006: James Harms

Library of Congress Cataloging-in-Publication Data
Gillett, Mary Jo Firth, date.
    Soluble fish / Mary Jo Firth Gillett.
       p. cm. — (Crab Orchard series in poetry)
    "First book award."
    ISBN-13: 978-0-8093-2773-7 (pbk. : alk. paper)
    ISBN-10: 0-8093-2773-2 (pbk. : alk. paper)
    I. Title.

PS3607.I444S65 2007
811'.6—dc22   2007004462

Printed on recycled paper. ♻

The paper used in this publication meets the minimum requirements of
American National Standard for Information Sciences—Permanence of Paper
for Printed Library Materials, ANSI Z39.48-1992. ∞

For Greg, Emily, Lincoln, and Elizabeth

For Dorothy G. Firth

In memory of Dennis Firth

Contents

Acknowledgments

My thanks to the editors of the following journals where these poems
first appeared:

CALYX—"Your Mouth"
Crab Orchard Review—"Like a Deity, Like a Diatom," "Snowflake
    Obsidian," "Spindrift"
The Driftwood Review—"The bag lady," "Every memory is a dream,"
    "Letter to the Muse"
The Eleventh MUSE—"Lighthouse"
The Florida Review—"Dad's Cornea Transplant," "Higgins Lake,
    Michigan, 9-11"
Green Mountains Review—"My Refrigerator, and Other Acts of Whim,
    of Faith," "Of Pavlov," "Segue"
Harvard Review—"Word"
The MacGuffin—"Watching Dad Filet a Bass," "What I Believe, with
    Four Final Words from Li-Young Lee"
Margie—"Fish Tales"
Michigan Quarterly Review—"World Enough"
Onset Review—"Cardinal," "Lightning Bugs," "A Note to the Skeptics"
Passages North—"Camping Out in the '50s"
The Southern Review—"Itch, Scratch," "Timeline for Lovers"
The Sow's Ear Poetry Review—"Valences"
Sycamore Review—"Chicken Tile," "Making Soup," "Memory," "On
    Being Asked by a Student How You Know When a Poem Is Done"
Third Coast—"Airborne," "I ask—," "Of Snakes, Of Gluttony"
Witness—"Sea Monkeys"

Poems in this collection have appeared in three chapbooks: *Not One*
    (Writer's Voice of Metropolitan Detroit, 1998 winner), *Tiger in a*
    Hairnet (Small Poetry Press Select Poets Series, 1999 winner), and
    Chandeliers of Fish (Poetry West, 2004 winner).

"Word," "Spindrift," "Memory," and "World Enough" appeared in *New Poems from the Third Coast: Contemporary Michigan Poetry*, edited by Michael Delp, Conrad Hilberry, and Josie Kearns, Wayne State University Press, Detroit, 2000.

"Word" was reprinted in *Century of Voices: Detroit Women Writers Anthology 1900–2000*.

"Sea Monkeys" was reprinted in *Slipstream* 25 (2005).

"Timeline for Lovers" was reprinted in *Driftwood Ludington Poetry Feast* (Special Edition, 2006).

"On Being Asked by a Student How You Know When a Poem Is Done" was reprinted in *Ludington Poetry Festival 2004*.

"What I Believe, with Four Final Words from Li-Young Lee" was reprinted on Verse Daily (October 31, 2002).

My deepest thanks to Robin Behn, Philip Dacey, Deborah Digges, James Harms, Patricia Hooper, Rick Jackson, Phillis Levin, Tom Lynch, David Rivard, and friends in Montpelier and Detroit for their sound advice and support.

Special thanks to Jon Tribble, Bridget Brown, Barb Martin, and Kathleen Kageff of Southern Illinois University Press for their expertise.

 *One*

A true confession: I believe in a soluble fish.

CHARLES SIMIC
from "The Minotaur Loves His Labyrinth"

Itch, Scratch

after Stephen Dunn

From everywhere and all-at-once,
from somewhere beneath the moon,
came the deep-sea fish that needed
to see, came the not-yet-flying squirrel
eyeing the too-far limb, came whale
and dolphin and bigger brains,
hair before razor, less fur more skin,
the opposable thumb, and fingers
for rings, for triggers, and of course
the triggerfish, though not in that order,

came bait-and-switch, lure and gulp,
the alligator snapping turtle,
came dog and god and much later
The Spanish Inquisition not-for-the-inquisitive,
came the rack and correct truths
and a need to stretch the truth,

and then a taller world—
upright posture before posturing—
came anger and angst and absinthe,
waistlines fat and thin, fancier hair and skin,
hook and eye in search of closure, exposure,
came style and stink and thus the harpoon,
and soon demigods and demitasse,
swagger and soiree, clipper ship and film clip,
and (without order) pit bulls, tar pits, cherry pits and pitfalls,
bells to sound joy, danger, and then

a complex of fears, because with neurons
come neuroses, bats in our belfry,
a lift from Zoloft, and learning to embrace
your beard of bees, your May your mayhem,
the hive of days honeycombed
with sweetness and stings.

Like a Deity, Like a Diatom

The bright fuchsia hibiscus, paper thin
and thinly veined but large as a dessert plate,
its secret parts suddenly in your face,

my young daughter at the toy store when she
grabbed the purple Pegasus with the jewel
in its belly and said, *I've wanted it all my life!*—

desire—elemental, sudden, but large as Pangea,
a single continental body not drifting into pieces
but straining toward some fine exaggeration,

a Rorschach, a fugitive embellishment, something
you never knew you'd waited for all your life.
Abundant in the energy of spawn and sperm,

imperceptibly persistent in diatoms
that leach silica from aquarium walls, prickly
yearning of cactus for rain, cosmic pull of tide to shore—

this wish to connect, to possess, so pervasive
I could almost be persuaded that an abandoned
bottle in a field begins to resemble the reeds,

fine grasses that surround it. Life a reaching out,
a time lapse film of flowers that bloom and fold,
bloom, fold morning and night, irrepressible pulse,

pointless delight less functional than a nose ring,
each breath sighing *on, on.* And no thinking about
fragility, Keats coughing blood at twenty-five,

chalk outlines, SIDS. Despite reality, always desire.
Even in the tight electronic arc of the TV screen,
life around the water hole, life in the Himalayas,

life even in the deep sea abyss, and lava
sizzling into an ocean to become a million billion
particles of sand, pixels swimming on this screen—

my longing that of the male silk moth
whose feathered antennae can distinguish
one molecule of pheromone from seven miles away.

Of Pavlov

Tidy, but toothed—like a tiger
in a hairnet—incongruous!—that's us.
Not the clockwork slip of gear to gear
but like pilots jettisoned from a cockpit,
wearing seatbelts for safety and pretending
there's no whirlwind eddy, no breathlessness,
just the familiar voice of the financial planner,
prepared for every eventuality. Uh-huh.
Tell that to Rufus Godwin whose fox-hunting dog
disappeared near Pensacola with the anti-theft
electronic collar still b-b-b-beeping, leading
trackers to the stomach of a 10' 11" alligator.
Imagine it—poor "Flojo" snapped up mid-howl
along the game trail. In all, seven collars found
inside the gator's insides, a muffled fugue, small
aftershocks of the canine wails that must've
sounded, to reptilian ears, like dinner bells—
everything being a matter of perspective—
like Captain Hook's nemesis,
the tick-tock of hungers that won't be quelled,
primitive croc and gator patrolling
billabong and bayou, taking on all comers,
all for the sake of the belly, of breeding—
not what my English grandmother meant
by that word. Ah, this torque of body and mind—
the growling stomach trying to keep time
with a wind-up metronome, winding down.
Darwin right, after all—what works works.
And what works will prevail, despite
the gator harpooned and trussed and slung

into a truck, jaws duct-tapped shut. Despite
the tenacity, the energy of that collar—
still going!—the toothed and leathery,
old, old hunger, utterly unimpressed by
electronics. Feel it—that swamp smell bellow.

Sea Monkeys

No one knew what they were but every kid
wanted them. Hyped in comic book ads,
they looked like goofy aliens, not monkeys.
Add a little water, and abracadabra
they'd be breast stroking their way into your life,
life from nothing, spontaneous as the famous
frog falls of Evansville, Indiana,
when a rainstorm became a downpour of frogs
the size of nickels, bouncing off umbrellas,
plunking into birdbaths, peeping and croaking
because they were very much alive
and far more vocal than that enormous
underground mushroom discovered in Michigan's
Upper Peninsula, celebrated on T-shirts,
There's a Humungus Fungus Amungus
the size of 35 football fields,
heavy as a blue whale, the biggest organism
on the planet, centuries of cloaked existence
lying imperceptibly beneath our feet
until Johann Bruhn stumbled upon it
as he studied the effects on plant life
of a buried U.S. Navy antenna
used to communicate with subs. So much
hidden activity, which even as a kid
I suspected, especially when I checked out
the graffiti under the viaduct,
the Rouge River gurgling past drawings
of figures primitive yet compelling
as the petroglyphs of New Mexico.
What I saw was a woman's body, frontal,
and a cannon in profile with roundish things,
wheels I decided, and a barrel-shaped chamber

from which issued a series of lively dotted lines
propelled vaguely toward the woman, toward
the space between her legs. It was captioned
The Big Bang which I found very confusing
but knew was important.
                              Years later, I asked a man
what it felt like to be aroused but confined
to his clothes. *A whale, it's like a whale—*
caught in a baggie, he grinned. *Sperm whale.*
I see the burgeoning in my own children,
wriggling into new worlds, fish never before
seen, risen from hidden depths—
coelacanth struggling in the net.

Pollywog

Children peddle them door-to-door, one to
my daughter who examines this mobile inkspot
daily, this piece of dark confetti,
this celebrant of life, sperm-like,
dimpling the water's surface. In a few days,
Look, look, she yells, *hands!* Obsessed with
metamorphosis, we pump oxygen in
with an airstone, cheering on the tiny life
until hind legs hoist its body onto a branch,
its pulsing throat a blur, its pinhead eyes
alert to new necessities. It must revise
its life. *Ants!* is the commandment
on my daughter's sticky notes. We pluck bugs
as gods might. A tongue shoots out,
the belly distends, and suddenly this being
smaller than the tip of my smallest finger,
this petite Buddha, smiling, inscrutable,
is a real toad in a not-so-imaginary garden.
I move the terrarium into the sun
and at night the stars shine down as they did
on the Turkish town of Kahramanmaras
the night of a recent lunar eclipse when
eight frightened men opened fire on the moon.
Daughter, you have been so lucky with this life,
but men's fears and joys leap unpredictably.
The human heart, that hooligan, that well-muscled
buccaneer, free-wheeling simpleton, burglar
of good sense given to sudden extravagance
this week was also moved to celebrate
21 thread-like stems flowering
on the compassionate eyebrow of Kuan Yin,

sacred Buddhist statue, flowers that bloom
only every three thousand years budding now,
inexplicably, on the gilded brow.

Memory

is the empty sock on the floor that still holds
the shape of the foot. It's a thin strip
of the entire picture, shredded by the eyes' sense
of event, the mind like Dan Rather on location
on the moon, a place with comparatively little
gravity yet clichéd and thus, like Swiss cheese,
full of holes. This business of thinking back
to a point in time is like writing a poem that
cites another poem. Dobyns does it—a man
explains to his wife that the Stevens line,
Let be be finale of seem, means *what exists is
more important than what seems to exist.*
Just goes to show how difficult it is to explain
the essentially evocative. What I want to do
is up the ante—write a poem that quotes a poem
that quotes a poem. Because that's exactly
the problem with memory. It's like those nesting
matryoshka dolls, the features of the smallest
so diminutive who knows what they really look like?
Just a semblance of the real, like Mount Rushmore.
Not really flesh, but hard and craggy, and much
much bigger than real life, and bigger is better,
right? The problem is that truth—read that memory—
is always in tension with a soluble fish. Yes,
like Simic, I believe in it—flux, not finale—
everything on the edge of becoming, ready
to slip into something else. Not like
dolls inside dolls inside dolls but children
holding a flashlight under a colander,
casting stars into a darkened room, each moment,
each breath, air in a windsock, spilling out.

Chicken Tile

The first time I saw my mother cry I was five or maybe six and being
careful not to step on the square tile in the middle of the kitchen floor.
It held the shape of a rooster with bright cockscomb and open red beak
that seemed to jump out at me. I tried not to look at it or at my mother

standing over the sink, her back to me, her narrow shoulders quivering
like the neighbor's collie who'd slunk home that night whining,
    his leather
leash dragging; and on Dixie Highway, the thin body of my
    eleven-year-old
neighbor sprawled flat in the rain in her cotton print dress. It was then

I knew that terrible things happen—for every thousand birds seen
swooping in perfect parabola, one is snagged by some sudden
    momentum,
some momentary lapse of impulse or instinct. And, walking home
on a bone-cold day in a white cocoon of snow, I was eight and
    hadn't thought

of my dead neighbor in months. Crossing Shea Avenue wrapped like
a mummy in my scarf, I heard the crunch of something heavy
rolling toward me. I jumped and the car fin barely caught my shoulder
spinning me around unhurt, but small and twirling and rigid as a little

ballerina in a jewelry box. Home again, I pulled off my heavy clothes
and the wet wool stink rose around me and the chicken's shiny
    black eye
stared; and I stared back hard at that stupid, gaudy bird placed
    so improbably,
so immovably in the square tile, flat in the middle of our kitchen floor.

Camping Out in the '50s

Half a bubble off level is all Dad would say
when neighbors spoke in hushes about Mrs. Gillis.
Mr. Burns said she had *a few screws loose*,
as if just a twist or two, what we learned in

Girl Scouts—right-tighty, lefty-loosey—
would fix her up. After all, it wasn't
quite normal to scatter the neighbor's garbage
on the street, to brandish a knife in the face
of the Fuller Brush man. She *was* one taco short
of a combination plate, but there was something

about that time that could drive a woman berserk,
her S.O.S. pads quietly rusting under the sink,
the promise of The American Dream rattling about
like a new-world poltergeist. Maybe I'm wrong,
maybe it was no different than today,

but I still get the willies when I think about
the little Gillis boy, how he fell astride
the edge of a window well, one leg in,
one out, the whole town whispering,
He'll never have kids, never pee normally,

my sense of normal remixed daily—
the vague scent of gun oil still playing about
my father's fingertips when he tucked me in,
someone else's Dad blitzed on Blatz
as he debated how far the barrel

should lead the duck before *lettin' 'er rip;*
and the sons crouched in trees
taking pot shots with BB's at anyone
who took a short cut along River Rouge.
Anyone was fair game. I hated being female.

But Harriet, Donna, how we loved your
pointlessness—it still makes me woozy.
Amazing we didn't all turn psycho, waiting, waiting
in mind-numbing boredom for something to happen.
It was a pretend world with a real button to push

and though I had to wear a sissy dress to school,
I'd run home, rip it off, then tear outside
to whup the boy next door. I was betwixt and between—
old enough to know about graffiti under the bridge,
young enough to wonder how anyone could do *that*—

except for Maribelle on the swing who'd
pump, pump her legs until, dress flying, she was
so high the whole world could see, well, everything.
It was the alpha decade of the atomic age,
caught in a blinding-light posture, a collective

duck-and-cover chassis in overdrive so cranked up,
so torqued, we were all slightly off kilter.
Even the kids. Hell, we loved to play high noon
in the backyard. Piled into a mildewed canvas tent,
we'd sweat it out, the air in there

ninety-five degrees Fahrenheit and rising,
like a rocket, like Jackie Gleason's arm,
anger, finger pointing skyward, his yeasty, almost
lusty voice screaming how he'd love to send her,
To the moon, Alice, to the moon!

Hand-Me-Down Pantoum

We saved everything—
used rubber bands, tissue paper, lunch bags.
Nothing was too small, too old.
We didn't have much—

used rubber bands, tissue paper, lunch bags,
Uncle John's grudge against the neighbors.
We didn't inherit much—
the family Bible and bad teeth,

Uncle John's grudge against the neighbors.
Ma grew snapdragons, Pa caught perch.
The family Bible and bad teeth
impressed us. Waste not, want not, we said—

Ma grew snapdragons, Pa caught perch.
Hellfire, McCarthy, and the KKK
scared us. Waste not, want not, we said,
canning peaches, mending socks.

Hellfire, McCarthy and the KKK—
fear ruled. God, the dirty commies, men in hoods.
Canning peaches, mending socks,
it was the post-war boom.

Fear ruled—God, the dirty commies, men in hoods.
Peggy Lee sang "It Ain't Necessarily So."
It was the post-war boom.
We were used to making do.

Peggy Lee sang "It Ain't Necessarily So."
We sang "Holy, Holy, Holy."
We were used to making do—
S&H green stamps, scraps for the compost.

We sang "Holy, Holy, Holy"
and saved everything—
S&H green stamps, scraps for the compost,
nothing was too small, too old.

Grandma's Fingerless Gloves

> Two things make a story. The net
> and the air that falls through the net.
> —Pablo Neruda

Crocheted, lacy, elegant, this loose network
of loop and knot. Who knows what consumed
the mind that worked the hook, the web

now a bit unraveled by time and a moth's hunger,
the design widened here and there into pea-sized
holes. I slide a glove on and my veins are rivers

running beneath that topography, that worn path,
that bumpy hillock we call family. I gently tug it
off, the limp and innocent sack of childhood,

the glove of deep sleep in the early years, one of
many second skins—grandmother, mother,
the young daughter I shouted to as she left

for school, *Have fun stormin' the castle!*
the words of Miracle Max in *The Princess Bride.*
And so it is the air falls through the net of our day,

the knowing references no one else will get,
the knot and loop of what one can know
of another, the startle, the pleasure in linkages

never recorded, the delicious web, and all
that falls through that net—a puff of air, a burst
soap bubble, a lover's breath on the neck.

Airborne

Daughter, you're so inventive—like Daedalus, Leonardo,
the Wright brothers—but opposite—conjuring a million ways
for flight to falter. And you're partly right. Up here,
if the engine sputters, you can't just pull over to the shoulder.

But I don't think of that as rooftops below me reflect
the first spears of light, mirrors nearly buried
in the crushed black velvet of a blouse from India
which I wear for its consoling touch—

as monopoly houses cluster about a sense of community,
the stifling cocoon of need, of what is safe, knowable—
as a family might gather about a campfire, or ancestors
hunker about a few embers at the beginning of human time.

Not so long after the tar pits, after the tarmac,
there is the safety video which no one watches,
which breaks down—an only remotely disturbing fact,
immersed as we are in small pillows, pc's, best sellers.

Suddenly, though, the film is back,
obsessing about procedures for unscheduled landings.
I am thoroughly attentive to my plastic glass
of Florida orange juice, not just for breakfast anymore

because almost nothing can be relegated to
a particular time, place. Despite the sunshine vitamin,
no place on earth—or above it—is immune.
Legionnaire's disease might strike anyone, each host

a ghost of what will be, taken in like a Trojan horse,
each body a house, a fortress, a speck,
a pulsing asylum traveling amidst roofs that glow at dawn
like the eyes of animals at night,

a strangely grounded constellation. The dome of the world
lies below, bony bowl with a string of lights familiar as
rhinestones at the neck of my grandmother who dressed
deliciously each night for dinner. All no more under my control

than this metal chrysalis, propeller sunlit, revolving
to create a frenetic line like the peaks, dips
on the graph of a lie detector. If I think about
the biggest lies I've ever told—

daughter, the truth is, there is so much horrendous,
splendid chaos, even those hollow-boned beings
genetically built and feathered for flight aren't safe—
the bird I hit on the freeway, a feathered explosion.

Segue

This night, anniversary of your birth,
I swirl dark chocolate icing into
spiral arms and think of things sexual,
spacial: black holes, the Big Bang,
star clusters spinning outward—
what Hubble had in mind—
distant galaxies speeding away
from the Milky Way without pause
as space, a black stretch-leotard
sprinkled with glitter, rides on one
gigantic inhalation—the way
everything reaches to extend itself,
ferns unfurling, nautilus moving
outward, its sealed chambers like
small time capsules but personal,
like the whorl on your thumb,
those papillary ridges
fingerprinting passage—
like that night I felt you swim up
from the tunnel that holds the curled form
easily, the way layers of sediment hold
a shell, or the way the throat
holds a word until sound bursts forth,
come-cry whose final faint reverberations
linger on the tongue like a vestigial tail.
I cannot say how we move between
worlds, dimorphic, our toes curved
into question marks, vernix fingers curled
like waxy shrimp—swimmer's hand sliding
from custom fit to custom fit,
glove of dark sea then air hugging it.

Lighthouse

I want to plant it in my head, a trigger,
a signal to call back that day,
the whole scene lit—
the once round face of my son angling
irrepressibly toward manhood, his lanky arms
salvaging bits of beach glass, how he squatted
then leapt after something jumping like
his Adam's apple—wrapped in the careful
topography of crouch, a soft frog caught
in its thin-skinned pouch, at first quieting
in the dark of his hands then slipping away—
the way a boy moves in determined
leaps, beyond choice, into a landscape where
raucous gulls dispute a crawfish claw
at the water's edge and the next wave, that
industrious maid, wipes away the water line—
foam, treasure, trash. All this not unlike
the way a child feels his days, floating
breathless *ands* without end. Or the way
his deepening voice and long limbs
will be tossed like debris tumbling over and over
until the smoothed edges slip past one another.
The fact of knowing doesn't change a damn thing—
the lighthouse vacant, the indifferent waves,
this day of breath on cold glass,
and two miles out, a red buoy blinking.

Fish Tales

Radtke, an avid angler, was fishing at 28-foot depths with
a lead-head jig rigged with a twister tail and a stinger-hooked
minnow on a four-pound line . . .

—Eric Sharp, *Detroit Free Press*

. . . and so Bob Radtke is surprised to find himself
struggling with a five-foot sturgeon hooked
while fishing for walleye on the Detroit River.
It's a cold April day and he clasps the fish tight
against his camouflage jacket before releasing it.
It is slippery as love and his chest heaves
for he's fought the fish for an hour, wearing it down
slowly while buddy Todd managed the trolling motor
to follow the biggest fish of Bob's life
two miles upstream to a spot near Mud Island.
And there's a picture to prove it because these are
modest men not braggarts, not given to exaggeration,
not like those characters on the fishing shows
columnist Sharp calls Two-Bubbas-in-a-Boat.
And if Stafford says writing is like fishing
and if Simic says he believes in a soluble fish,
I guess Radtke could tell us a thing or two about
dropping a line into the depths for whatever might come
and how easily a 4-pound test line can snap,
the fish dissolving right in front of your eyes.
I must admit I believe in fish stories—ice fishermen
who stick their frozen catch upright in the snow
to form a pike-and-perch picket fence around the shanty,
a hint of home even in the wild. And how those fish,
thawed, have been known to come to life in the very face
of the filet knife. *Life will find a way,* says Goldblum
in *Jurassic Park*. There's the bamboo shark in Motown's

Belle Isle Aquarium, after years without a mate
giving birth. Who knew? Fact is, I owe my very life to fish,
to fish luck. Catch, and release. In '42 my not-yet-father
on leave in Australia, the fish wild for the bait and he so keen
on catching them that, unlike his buddy, he decides
not to sign up for duty on the coveted new sub.
On its maiden run, never again heard from. Old timers
will tell you it's all just fish luck. What lures you, hooks you,
reels you in. What magnanimous hand lets you go.

 *Two*

       ...I

Like to think that this fishing-tackle

Was left behind by those Japanese fishermen

Whom they have now driven from the West Coast into camps

As suspect aliens, that it came into my hands

To keep me in mind of so many

Unsolved but not insoluble

Questions of humanity.

BERTOLT BRECHT
from "The Fishing Tackle"

I ask—

because everything turns on the moment, its timing—
the firefly smashed on the windshield,
the final fading of its chemical glow—
and because the veins in our hands even now
rise through skin like ridges on a pine handrail, well-worn—
you, close to me as words to a page, did you know—
in our lifetime the whole North American continent
will have drifted eastward roughly the length of my body?
No wonder it's so difficult to find each other.
You said your Aunt died young but reconciled—
or did you say happy—because she'd seen the world,
all but six countries, travel a balm for death.
I can almost share it, your enthusiasm for place,
the iambs of places you've been—
Peru, Nepal, Zaire, Bhutan—
we count them off like minutes, like expectant mothers
counting days. I want to pretend that time
is not the point, that how we frame it
is all that matters, but this shard box on my desk,
its lid a piece of Ming pottery—
a piece of sky fixed in place—is only a remnant,
unlike the earthworms I dig for my daughter's garter snake,
or how he gulps them down in honest greed,
their struggle futile but somehow touching.
Yet, who can believe even what is seen?
In a bayou the mother alligator hungrily
mouths her children, cradling them in her tight cave,
her stalagmite teeth a picket fence. She is as intent
as blue jays who every spring build a nest
at the corner of my porch. There is nothing
to anchor the sticks to except each other—
they fall and fall. So much for instinct.

Words are no better. Bedtime, I hold my daughter
as she sobs, *I don't want to die, I don't want you to die.*
What can I say? It is like those times
when the cry at the peak of loving
so defines my borders I can only fall into movement,
think small, back and forth—
spring, when I sweep the twigs from the porch—
no words, only this nest of now, and now.

Word

Not just a syllable, a ululation, click, roll, slur, trill. I want
the whole damn thing, the roller-coaster ride of consonant, vowel,
accent and innuendo. I want serendipity do-da, I want somnambulant
rapture, and I want it mal, bad—malcontented, maladjusted,
    maloccluded.
I want it alpha and penultimate—there is no end. I want the sound
and everything it conjures up, the surprise—that wasp nest
still clinging to the eaves of memory, thin paper that seems empty
but buzzes to life with a little warming—or should I say warning—
a little onomatopoeic poltergeist in my head, a haunting, a mesh
of sound and moment, fit tight as tiles in a Moroccan mosaic,
or the cowry shell wrapped about its softer insides, the subtle
pianissimo of what it is—these sounds our companions, linking us
one to another like some species specific duet—or should I say
diet—the panda and its bamboo, the koala and its eucalyptus, how
things are joined as, when I say a word—veranda, for example—
or a name, Einstein—it never means strictly what I want it to
because of the baggage, everything it ever was—including
    the madness—
everything the seine net of memory can hold—squirming shiners,
bits of vegetation, muck and grit and algae—the small, the smell of it,
so that even now, dry and propped against the garage, this net teems,
the wind catching at its webbing, the primal smell like bedsheets
after sex—a skin, a skein of sound, whirl of x and y, both cargo
and carriage—like any word—part cure, part tremor at the core.

Poem for the Hibiscus

It has been said the flowering hibiscus
is the lover you cannot refuse. The soil trembles,
even the seventeen-year-locust cannot wait.

The blooming hibiscus is a banquet—
dictionaries rush to redefine hunger.
(The hibiscus knows salivation and salvation
are the same bud, opening.)

A hibiscus bloom can stop traffic,
even in Rome.
Even in Rome
the dog does not pee on the hibiscus.

The genes of the hibiscus harken back to China.
To be late because one has admired the hibiscus
is not to be late.

The flowering hibiscus is quietly subversive.
There were many private conversations with Gandhi.

When hibiscus blooms sway in the wind,
shackles on the ankles of prisoners know
they are in the wrong line of work.

The physics of the opening hibiscus
is a thousand tuning forks in sympathetic vibration.
The ruby-throated hummingbird hums louder.

When the chameleon, hibiscus, and scarlet macaw
write a paper, it is on color theory.
The genre, creative non-fiction.

Some day there will be a line of lingerie
composed entirely of hibiscus petals.
At the least provocation
the petals will drop away.

Cardinal

A man repairs my neighbor's chimney
on a day brilliant as a young child,
as a child is brilliant in the world,
each morning waking as if he expects
this sudden feathered comma of color
which distracts the man on the roof
so that he staggers, not falling but
flailing his arms long enough to remind me
it is not the job of beauty to save us.
I've heard that even asleep, behind
red-rimmed lids, we're still on nightshift
working unfinished business. My youngest
once told me that in her dreams she beats up
authority figures. Violent, but otherwise
perfectly reasonable. After TV news—
totems of bodies, explosions, weather,
a newborn crying from a dumpster—
how easily I then think of the cedars
at the side of my house broken by snow,
or the red azalea I thought half-dead
now in full bloom—this, then this
jumble clamoring to be taken in,
cruel, erotic as the thorns used to nick
the back of a Dinka woman, the web
of intricate welts a braille of beauty
to be fingered by her lover—
more than skin deep—
like this scar on my daughter's chin,
months old, still red, already
teaching her how quickly
the narrow tire of joy is overturned.

Higgins Lake, Michigan, 9-11

The hollow coo of a dove lassoes
me in a rope of song, a tightening lure
cocooning about me as if to soothe
with a feathery whisper so familiar
the voice might be yours or mine
or one in a chorus scattered wide
as the waves, numberless as the sighs
imbedded in us, murmurings we ride
at the edge of the day, steady as the tick-tock's
uncoiling. Something to put your faith in.
Almost a religion. Or a dirge, a wake
of voices never to be heard again, thin
exhalations of night wind against the dock.
Who is to say what makes a hymn?

Farmer, 1938

after Ben Shahn's *Sunday Painting*

A slight man stands in a field in the Midwest
in his Sunday best—white shirt and suspenders,
black hat with grosgrain ribbon at the crown.
He could have been one of my grandfathers
though they were "men of the cloth," not farmers,
and this man is no particular man.
Bushy eyebrows protrude from under the brim,
his head turned from you so you cannot see
his face, his eyes. He is the kind of man
who is not aware of you or even interested
in how you see him, which is only in profile.
What strikes you is his stance, his outline
against the landscape, though "against" isn't right.
In this fallow field of dry grass, sandy loam,
bits of scrub growth, he is neither a part of the field
nor apart from it. He is not yet old, not yet grey,
though there is a spread at his middle
and a slump to his shoulders from leaning
into the wind. Here, even in his Sunday clothes,
he is not out of place. In fact, he wears this place
comfortably, his thoughts taking on the hue
of the sky as crickets chorus the dusk,
his stride stirring up bright clouds of fireflies.
Hands clasped at his back, one hand stands out
enormous, out of proportion, because
one's desires always exceed one's grasp.
He seems at peace, perhaps thinking about
his strapping sons, the world's progress, the descent
of the Bathysphere 3,048 feet into the Atlantic.

It is the year of the ball-point pen. Three years before
Pearl Harbor, before mushroom clouds, even
before we found those cave paintings in France.
He is alone but not lonely. He kicks at a clod of dirt.
The land stretches out, endless before him.

Dear Departed Reverend Grandfathers,

there's no way to explain my wallowing
  in fields of burdock, goldenrod, yarrow,
the lure of rocks that hide slime-pathed slugs,
  pillbugs, dewy leaves that prism sunlight
into muted stained-glass Sundays I still carry,
  close as a pocket, familiar as a tongue,
my child eyes and ears infused with spectacle,
  thin voices singing as hands pantomimed,
This little light of mine, I'm gonna let it shine,

  a wish to hold, to shape the world
as we passed that brass collection plate
  up and down the pews of the few who knew
beyond a shadow of a doubt what was what,
  palms proffering wine and wafer, mouths little O's
closing on metaphor—sight and sound beyond sense—
  the sheer pressing opulence of cattail, cane,
chicory, the blood love of my children,
  the deep sweet oblivion of skin on skin,
invisible as Venus in daytime.

  Grandfathers, where are you in this restless
flurry of taut-ribbed leaves turning in wind,
  quackgrass, timothy, bulrush rising in
roadside and field? In the irrepressible green,
  somewhere beyond my own embroideries,
what thin strand in chlorophyll and red cell,
  in amoeba and sperm whale, in the complex
turnings of unseen meiosis, gamete straining
  for replication, threads through all
like the drawstring of an enormous bag?

Watching Dad Filet a Bass

The first time I saw him do it I became a believer,
I thought he'd missed his calling. He could have been
a priest performing the sacrament, his movements
were so deliberate, so purposeful, like a ritual.

First a quick sure cut to the head above the eye
but back a bit, about where the forehead would be
if there'd been a forehead, then everything—the red gills
flashing like tiny rhythmic fans, the methodically

gulping jaws, the wet flat slap of the delicate tail—
everything stopped as the spiny fins folded quietly in.
Then he stuck the knife in beneath the chin
or where a chin should be, making a quick

sure slice down the opalescent belly shimmering
like a sequined gown. The roe, entrails spilled out
in a well-packed, orderly fashion as my mother's words
rose strangely inside me, a place for everything,

everything in its place. Even the disemboweling was impressive.
The knife paused, hanging in midair, and I thought of the way
the lid rolls back on a sardine can as he peeled the flesh
from the skin for a neat boneless filet, the creamy white meat

packed in tidy rows—organized—almost intelligent.
He wiped the fillet knife delicately, testing its edge
with his thumb the way a barber might check his straight razor
before a shave. I shuddered, and he must have misunderstood:

I like to think their system's too primitive to feel a thing,
he said. *But the catfish are the worst. They cry like babies*
when you pull them from the water . . . I mostly throw them back.
He didn't see—it wasn't the blood or the detached, cool way

he handled his tools, or even death that transfixed me.
I saw him revealed, altered by necessity. I saw the way
need shapes us, how it brings together flesh and steel
with hardly a slip.

Valences

Funny how a sudden flash of flesh
can jolt you, transport you back
to first grade and James who liked
to stick his finger and other things
out his fly. It happened again as I was
sitting in my van waiting for the light
to change. I heard a honk and saw a man
nodding and gesturing and pointing to
his phallus which stood up in front
of his steering wheel like a new species
of thick-stalked mushroom, lost
and looking for its field. The view
was incongruous, implausible as a fine marble
statue, say Michelangelo's *David*, suddenly
colorized. I was reminded in a rush
of other scenes blatant as two dogs humping
on the front lawn, enhancements drawn by
young artless hands, beads of the mysterious
strung together to be fingered in odd moments,
a sort of risqué rosary of the mind—pairs
of benippled breasts staring like little half-lidded
eyes and disembodied penises-in-space floating
hopefully in odd places, little rockets
proclaiming what they could do, where they
could take you. Strange how it all becomes
a part of you—oh, not you, exactly,
but a hint, a suggestion of a realm we move toward,
the way those tinkertoy atoms in chemistry
were right, but wrong. The parts were there,
but too rigid, too literal, entirely missing
the most fundamental fact—the atom's willingness

to exchange, the electron's location only
a rough approximation within a realm
of probability, a best guess, a possibility.

Snowflake Obsidian

I'm drunk on slowness—
the pause of the fiddlehead fern
as it prepares to uncurl,
the intake of breath
a moment before the word,
the gathering of air and skill,
luck and intent to capture
the iced window's feathery moment
as our aviary hearts race
toward a much warmer convergence
of mis-matched pieces
wrapped in newsprint—
crystal bowl, stinky fishhead—
and who cares which of us is which?
a melding, like the black polished rock
with translucent white spots.
I must love you slowly, in caesura,
because Kundera is right,
the degree of speed is directly proportional
to the intensity of forgetting.
I love you the way I love
graffiti, our past tense—
there is a tenseness to it—
haunting us like an amputee's phantom pain
whenever the undertow, underworld
submarine captain in us shouts
Dive! Dive! into the abyss.
For love makes us
beggar and barbarian,
no more refined than the shaggy lapdog
across the street straining at his leash,
pulled by a heady concoction of reasons

beyond reason, your unsteady hand
on my skin, the field of spreading fire
what I silo in this world
of hitman and mannequin,
hovel and cathedral.

Of Snakes, Of Gluttony

I've heard the potato is exotic,
that it originally came from Peru
born of a pre-Columbian culture
rich in peanuts and warrior-priests.

I don't know if this is true
but I believe it. It adds flavor,
phyllo-layers of history and place,
Neruda's continent of the coiled

anaconda, *rapacious, religious,*
gigantic. Though possibly there are
no anaconda in Peru, it doesn't matter—
gluttony isn't interested in accuracy.

It's differences I crave, the many
kinds of potato—red and Idaho,
au gratin, French fried—I eat them all—
like swallowing an egg whole,

everything taken into the jaws,
the jaws my continent of sound,
long-vowel I and generous pi—
a tail of numbers twisting through

generations longer, Szymborska has said,
than the longest snake. Insatiable,
immense. Inexplicable as love.
I love the inexplicable—

this world where joy is still possible
despite history's lessons—how we torture
our neighbors and eat our enemies.
Despite the Humpty-Dumpty vertigo

of our hearts, always the helium hope
that something will happen. A bacchanalian
gambol on the green, Brueghel's rotund
bodies stomping, codpieces rising to

motion and rhythm like the heads of
curious cobras. Life is like that—surprisingly
inflatable. The used air that took refuge
in my lungs now bellows past cilia

and rose-petaled gills to snake its way
to a fetus where it bubbles—part star,
part amoeba, light that shouts and cell
that gropes across laboratory slide

as I grope now to say it—how we take in
the stringy syllables, this pulsing cord,
to send it out again. I hold it here,
bell and clapper, mouth and tongue.

A Note to the Skeptics

Don't tell me it makes no sense to say
the stroke of a child's eyelash against
my cheek is the touch of the blade
as I free the potato from its skin—

the stroke, how close I bring it in, so like
his whiskers against my skin telling me
all I need to know of pleasure, of pain,
and which I prefer, so that I keep the blade

at bay. Wedded to life, what else is there
but an oddball wacko longshot, a "take"
on the moment as I pass it? If I imagine
floating in a dinghy, madly bailing,

why not be Thor Heyerdahl high on his balsa,
rafting past archipelago, mangrove,
tidal shoreline, and blue-footed booby?
past the voice-over of Hitler's *Mein Kampf*,

and a pock-marked sea of atrocity,
past the fact that though I might want
champagne and filet mignon what I get
is Coke and meatloaf. So don't tell me

it's nothing—the sublime slant of this
extraordinary light hitting the trilobite
I keep on my desk to remind me,
take it in before it's gone.

Don't tell me happiness is irrelevant—
because there is death in the Dead Sea,
there is no beauty, no life in Yosemite?
There was the Spanish Inquisition,

there is whimsy—an armada of piñatas
without which I'm a curled armadillo,
a snail within its shell. What is there
but to be lashed to the mast,

to take my chances with the sirens?
What but to lighthouse the landscape,
foghorn the night, each note a sweet tattoo
of me, you—a torture, a Bible, a feast.

The bag lady

was a flea market find,
an old chandelier, a fox-headed wrap,

a gilt-edged book gone damp,
a classic, a wreck with presence—
Miss Havisham of Brush Street.

Inviting as chapped lips,
a late night at the morgue,
a high pier with loose boards.

But not dangerous.
Still, she gave me the heebie-jeebies.
That's why I studied her. To forget her.

Now, like bad genes, she's back.
Not déjà vu at all. More like
a sharp word, a bad back,

the familial past—subliminal trash
persistent as the mothball reek of Auntie's
closet. You'd like it to let you go,

but you are its breath,
its canary in the mine,
its reluctant gourmet.

You taste it, it sustains you.
You hesitate but it's essential—
the thirsty man's dirty glass.

I drink her in. An aged
Venus-on-the-half-shell,
up to her elbow in a dumpster,

hoping to add to her cache.
Hope is a dirty rag.
I didn't even say hello.

Hotel, Soldiers Field Road, Boston

Like swimming into a warm current in a northern lake,
these stars,

from the window of a Daystop Inn,
unexpected as the sense I've had

that I could have loved a stranger just for one small gesture,
just for being in a particular moment.

I cannot guess what conflation of light, body, place will be
the antidote for this sluice of days—what will stir me

from numbness. Tonight it's a sound—chink-clink—
man searching a dumpster for bottles, cans worth

five cents each. But it could have been anything—
a milk-carton-waxed-museum of missing children,

or smaller—the Cuban bee hummingbird
weighing less than one teaspoon of sugar.

Small losses . . .

as if yesterday's withered clematis
and the hollow space in the chrysalis
after the monarch's flown were moot points,
minor diminishments, ripples, blips, specks,
insignificant as the luster lost,
iridescence blown from a blue morpho's wing
in the evening breeze. As if the deepening
of the skin's chiseled lines, the delicate
crow's feet at the corners of a lover's eyes
were beneath notice. As if we could forget
how fallen fruit and the cheeks of an old friend
are kin, the deepening to fleshy sinkholes
proving how dependable it is—Time—
that constant companion slowly prying
the sweet meats loose, back-stabber at work
with a nut-pick, even on my own children,
those once tiny tyrant-kings, vagabond souls,
little hoboes bound to grow. How I hovered,
ready to tickle them from sleep, remembering
the shrill sound of fledglings fallen from a nest
at the roof's edge, small bodies plummeted
through a hole into the narrow unforgiving
space between walls. For days their peeping grew
weaker, weaker as their frantic delicate nails
scratched against rough plaster, against whatever
it was they knew of their slow plunge from light.

Ladybug

I was reading Neruda late into the night,
hoping to siphon off something for myself,
when she landed on my open notebook.

Not a real ladybug but an orange-spotted
imposter who picked her way in a drunken
waddle along the metal spiral, stopping

to sample a trace of something invisible
to me. She clambered inside the wire binding
to scuttle along the ditch of wide-ruled paper,

emerging at the end dissatisfied, it seemed.
The small pretender then left the page to fly
in loopy indirection to my open *New Yorker*.

She seemed to have a taste for Galway, lusty
insomniac marveling at the woman beside him,
her hank of hair and *the heat a slender body*

ovens up around itself. Understandable, the draw
toward warmth in a shivery spring. Each year
masses of fake ladybugs awaken to find

a secret way into the old cottage, only to then
die in prodigious numbers. I sweep mounds
of their dead shells from floor and sill

and sometimes take the living outside,
though I tire of even that short trek. Time
is short, and the journey full of cul-de-sacs

and dead ends. Above me, lured by the light she could not resist—listen—the click-click of insistent wings, little Icarus bumping against the bulb.

Letter to the Muse

Insistent beast! furry foot
in my door, jaws locked

on my most vital parts,
there are whole moments

when I don't care a whit
for you. But still you angle

your way in, sucker growth
at the base of a rambling rose.

Or else you take me by surprise,
quick as a rebel hand moves

from alms box to Kalashnikov.
And if you are like a lover,

old troll, you are a master
of bondage—the Marquis

had nothing on you. But
where are you today, old

unreliable, old shaky banister
on the steep stair, one moment

drought, the next monsoon, my
starvation, my feeding station,

yesterday's failed field,
tomorrow's bumper crop.

# Three

Over a dark railing, I watch the minnows, thousands, swirl
themselves, each a minuscule muscle, but also, without the
way to *create* current, making of their unison. . .

                          . . . making of themselves a
visual current, one that cannot freight in sway by
minutest fractions the water's downdrafts and upswirls, . . .
              motion that forces change—
this is freedom. This is the force of faith. Nobody gets
what they want. Never again are you the same. The longing
is to be pure. What you get is to be changed. More and more by
each glistening minute. . .

JORIE GRAHAM
from "Prayer"

Making Soup

I stir this broth, I think of the water snake,
skin finely braided, bark-textured, prehensile
tail wrapped around a branch like a monkey's
or marsupial's. How like a branch it looked!
Body stiff and straight, rigid as rigor mortis.
Few things in life as simple as its sudden lunge
with huge unhinged jaws, the marrow seeping from
these bones—basic needs, indigent residents
of the body, the things we notice, what we taste
and pronounce delicious as—I confess—the loneliness
when you left. Standing on the porch at three A.M.,
thinking about your 747, the impossibly
steep angle of its liftoff, the wild roar of engines,
earth shaking, all those gravity-defying lives
balanced inside, at first I thought I trembled from
the cold, or from my solitude, but now I see how
phallic the image was—read it again—
I was "thinking about your 747, the impossibly
steep angle of its liftoff, the wild roar of engines,
earth shaking, all those gravity-defying lives
balanced inside." Maybe you smile now at
comparative dimensions, but I tell you it is
the primordial soup, the possibility of the moment,
that keeps me fed, whole—the cracking chrysalis,
the infant curled to the mother's curve,
the body's periphery melting, even Heisenberg
shouting *Aha!* when he knew that the instant
we study even the subatomic moment we alter it.
I want to be that snake like an infant gumming
a nonverbal moratorium on thinking. I would be
the musk turtle, neck extended, nudging his mate
with a piggy snout, his toenails locked to the edge

of her shell. I have seen them infinitely patient,
adrift in the slow rock heave of love until finally
she scuttles to the corner of the tank, goldfish
nibbling at her carapace, and he floats upward,
the three keels of his back plate cutting the water,
his underbelly's skin white, goose-bumpy,
soft as our own pale flesh in the dark after love,
light sifting through the narrow metal strips
of miniblinds, our bodies slivered with moonlight.

Poppy Field, Lily Pond

Once in a while I'm drawn to those
unpeopled landscapes, unsullied vistas,
pristine gems inviting you to dream
yourself into the picture, a world
before the fall, before expulsion,
before words held back or wrongfully spoken
to the travel agent who didn't call back
because she wrote your number down wrong
again, and there goes your chance at Eden,
a greenly intimate world even The Jolly Green Giant
and the buyer for English Gardens can't
collaborate to create. A picture-perfect world
where ponds have no scum, flowers no bugs,
gardens no weeds. A world where you will
never be intimidated by the IRS,
never see misers bent lasciviously
over their ledgers. Where there will never be
a 19th century Russian soldier
leaning on his good arm, bleeding the snow red,
a young woman, or is it the bugle boy,
trembling beneath his coat. Where there will
never be a girl with a watering can
who's reached too far to scoop up a water lily.
No tragic billowing of her skirt like some
uncatalogued blossom. Here the palpably
beautiful canvas is a blank canvas,
the profusion of poppies a tabula rasa,
land before ruin, before limits where,
alone and quiet as night fog, you hope
to forget the hard look you gave your beloved,
the look that said, *Have I ever known you?*

What I Believe, with Four Final Words from Li-Young Lee

I believe there is no freedom
but the kite will tug at the string anyway.

I believe in the ditch but also the cattail
and the red-winged blackbird, the body
balanced and bobbing on a stem.

I believe there is always birdsong
but no one hears it all the time;
I believe sometimes there is no song—

I believe we exist to subvert what we believe.

I believe in the feral cat tense on its haunches,
the soft pleasure of its electric fur.

I believe when the lights go out, and they will,
the waters of Niagara still pound.

I believe lovers, even when they are afraid,
make good use of the dark.

I believe in the bodacious mind—the fear,
the exhilaration, the tenacity. And the bruises.

I believe a kiss will not make it all better
but might make it worthwhile.

I believe in the locomotive engine of the past,
its heft, its power, the shadow it casts.

I believe in the hairball, and other reasons
for ambivalence.

I believe in disparity—the Grand Canyon
and the paper cut.

I believe in acts of free will, the mind in freefall.

I believe every moment is manifold.

Electric Tomato

Life for the electric tomato is life on the edge—
the power comes from its roots, the spark from its juice.

The electric tomato is seedless which accounts
for its rarity—conditions have to be perfect.

The e.t. has one outlet but no ground fault interrupter.
Do not stick a fork in the electric tomato.

The electric tomato is a study in incongruity.
No one owns it, many would steal it.

Other garden vegetables are jealous,
especially the Beef Steaks and Big Boys.

The electric tomato admires the beauty of the hibiscus
but not its narcissism.

Because its politics are liberal, the electric tomato
does not deny the existence of a soluble fish

even though the electrical engineer denies the existence
of the electric tomato.

When my beloved says I shock him, I blame it on
you know who.

He points out that the electric tomato
masquerades as a vegetable but is really a fruit.

Do not attempt to pick the electric tomato.
Not for a salad, not for soup, not even for salsa.

The electric tomato is both electric and organic
but it only comes in red.

My Refrigerator, and Other Acts of Whim, of Faith

Like dating without sex or
religion without grace, my
hunger. Soon to be sated
by creamy tortellini
plunged into boiling water,
small pirouetting faces,
hats crimped close. But one's become
unglued, the edges flaring—
the winged hat of a flying
nun. I see it swell like some
tender tissue. How can it
be so suggestive, this plain
androgynous food? I could
further inflate the pasta,
make it religious, even
ridiculous—unhinged, or
lewdly aerodynamic.

Though if this frig is about
anything at all, maybe
it's about hope which isn't
a winged thing or the worship
of maculate perfection
but just a lot of waiting
around for redemption. The
right conditions. Ready as
a primed catapult yearning
for the merest movement, the
wriggle of a rope, mild mold's
reincarnation—Voilà,
penicillin! Let's hear it
for the strange fermentations

of leftovers left to their
own devices. Who knows what
lurks under the guise of the
unredeemed? Though it may sound
extravagant, bold, absurd
to say it, when hasn't food
been a sacrament? These cold
contents symbolic as—I
will say it—tortellini!—
so like love, like poetry,
which a dear devout friend once
said must be my religion.

On Being Asked by a Student How You Know
When a Poem Is Done

after Dean Young

I say three-and-a-half hours for medium rare
or when the juices run clear. If you prefer sweets,
when the syrup reaches the hard crack stage.
I say, when your childhood backyard becomes
the Garden of Eden and innocence becomes
an electric tomato, all juice and spark.
I say, when the time spent equals the emotion felt.
Wait. Reverse that.
I say, if you've been standing in a thunderstorm
half the night and all you've gotten is wet.
If you've written a baboon into a love poem
it might be time to stop. Or not.
I say, check the poem for *chandeliers of fish*,
the shimmer factor. Then I shrug and say
what Valery said. (At some point even
O Captain, My Captain abandoned ship.)
I say never stop until you've achieved *zpxtflo*,
unattainable zpxtflo. At least we've established
that. I say, when you've given up searching
for something to rhyme with orange because
you've eaten the orange. I think of Jarrell,
a sense of innate order when *the poem*
takes the place that has awaited it. I say
the poem might be done when the seventeen
whooping cranes following an ultralight
twelve hundred miles from Wisconsin to Florida
realize it's not one helluva big bird.
Then I tell my student what Deborah told me—
you must put on your leather jacket and go into
the cave. Even when the poem bares it fangs.

Maybe the poem's done when the stake of imagination
has been driven through the Frankenstein
of intent. I say the poem's done
when form and chaos get in bed together.

·

Timeline for Lovers

As if it were linear—
the fall of Tikal and the survival
of the Great Wall,

our evolution from amoeboid
to Sigmund Freud merely The Past,
post Magna Carta, MagnaDoodle.

As if we were not teetering
on the reef, the roof, the woof!
of what has come before us.

As if what grabs our attention
didn't feed our confusion,
G-string and G-force holding hands

as if there were a cosmic logic
to chiffonier and grenadier,
San Andreas Fault and no-fault,

Machu Picchu and Yabba-Dabba-Do!
As if it were orderly, mandated,
made some kind of perfect sense when

my barnacle-encrusted heart,
my mind just this side of the loony bin,
my banshee spirit, invite you in.

Animal!

The meandering centipede unwisely
surfaced as I watered my ficus.
Twisting below my shadow,
I saw it try to elude The Hand,
fleshy Cessna with no plans to pull up,
instrument that earlier passed a brush
through my daughter's long hair.
How quickly the heart goes haywire,
fist-sized pacifist pump falling suddenly
from a sleepy *hey-nonny-nonny-hum*
to machine of grim intent—
spirit of guillotine, quiet
scythe in irrevocable free fall—
as if it were my survival at stake.
How territorial, how absurd!
my over-eager heart booming tribally,
deaf to all but its own red sound,
murderous, urgent,
all rational thought lost
as a lone stripe might be on the flank
of a zebra as the herd thunders past.
Understand—I was determined to kill
that scout, that leggy interloper,
though it seems ridiculous—
I vie for space with a bug?
It was ugly. Threatening. And
how inventive each can be,
cloaked in camouflage, imperceptibly
aggressive as a river parasite
following a stream of pee
to the small opening of its host—

each urge of bug, bacteria, beast
the pure, unadulterated will to be.
Nothing personal.

Every memory is a dream

we speak of as if, upon waking,
it were possible to tease the hide
from the musculature, the soft pelt pried
from its softer inner workings, taking
care to keep the wild psychic beast alive,
each derring-do and Kumbaya corseted
to the honeyed past, to a hunger never sated
for the small voices buzzing in their waxy hive—
jeweled tormentors, the tickle of what was.
Addicted to the stings we felt, we gave,
we are sticky with the lives, loves we would save.
Restless beasts licking whiskers and claws,
tongues eager, teeth bared, we jostle and shove,
ripping each cell open, for beauty, for love.

Your Mouth

for Ernestine Augusta Gillett

I wanted the simplicity, the faith
of childhood rituals, the talismans
to ward off fear—a rabbit's foot,
a lucky penny, whatever it took
to make me believe you were safe.
I wanted the chants, the words we use
to ward off fear, the rhymes—
sidewalk cracks and mothers' backs,
sticks and stones and broken bones,
and names that could never hurt me.

But there was no ritual,
no chant, no training for this.
Not even in the practiced horror
of jungle movies where streams
teamed with implacable piranha
and paths were pocked by impartial
quicksand, each grain equally eager
to swallow a man, to close on lips
silent and seamed as a stone.
We should have known.

But nothing prepared us, you or me,
for this, name it, the sarcoma,
this cancer cold and white
as the marbled moon, this little
bloodless body balanced in your lungs.
No charm could save you
from the dark quiet waiting,
the terrible swollen feet and face

as you melted into your skin,
into your frame, by inches.

And when you whispered,
I had hoped to be around
to see what the kids would do,
your words sealed the space of years
and I was a child again in my fear,
whistling in the dark, crying
at the top of my lungs for your voice,
your lips, now closed as a peony bud,
the cool white petals packed like
unturned pages in your mouth.

Dad's Cornea Transplant

Something, maybe the music on the hospital PA—
soothing and old, those big band sounds
that spun sex on the 78, women's long hair
loose and wavy, Fred and Ginger at the Bijou—

something transported Mom, girlish again,
dreamy, telling me how they met at a dance,
how he moved slowly toward her in a baggy suit.
And I knew what she'd say next—

she didn't have nylons because, remember,
it was just after the war, so she knew
he'd ask her friend to dance, the one who wore
hose, seams traveling up the back of her legs,

up under her skirt. But she remembers
he turned instead toward her, and her laugh is
bare white legs barely touching the crease
in his gabardine pants, their two sets of feet

straining at the sharp right angles, the box step
tracing the shapes of the parquet floor,
their bodies the tug of a tethered kite.
What an artist might show with a glint of white

in the iris, the eye alert to the merest gust of wind
rippling the lake, a black bass in the shadow
of the dock, the sweep of its tail and delicate fins
holding its place against the current.

Lightning Bugs

Our home continents may be
an ocean apart, but on warm nights
when I watch these living embers flash
their shorthand message, I know
the light of dead and distant stars
shoots through both our geographies.
Despite dichotomies—
my Northern pines, your leguminous
acacias, my drifting fog, your
sun, implacable—the shapes are
constant, the outward manifesting
the inward. And what a composite
of meander, twist, and sphere we are,
my pea vine wrapping its helix coil
to your florets which strain like
clover toward the honeyed cell.
So, tell me again how you will lie at last
separate, discrete as each grain of sand
that blows across the face of Ozymandias,
and I will tell you how the ridges
of a shell press home its signature,
the spiraled arc of imprint not
just an encounter but memory
that lies deep in the vast space
of each atom—your hand pressing
the small of my back to you, the nape
of my neck and coil of my hair cupped
to your other palm as stars wink out
and the searching symmetries of our bodies
believe that this, this is the only revenge.

Spindrift

What hasn't already been said about
the moon, the stars? And though, Love,
we are no heavenly bodies, no constellations,
in our eyes there still lingers the light—somehow—
of a collapsing star, light too dim to pierce
these onion days. But see how the very world
works for us, nothing wasted, nothing lost—
each tear that slips to the anonymity of collar
or floor, each molecule of rain that seeps
to alligator sewers, I've read
once coursed the points of pyramids,
knew the likes of Cleopatra, and
after a season of spindrift or snow will
melt again to hot sands, thirst that is
sudden artesian and slow Paleozoic,
tiger's teeth and trilobite's scuttle across salt seas,
both larger than the sky's red giant,
smaller than the radium atom emitting its lethal dose
to Madame Curie. In this time, both briefer
than the engineer's nanosecond and longer,
much longer than the 100 million years
it has taken us to get to this moment, stripped
of its coverlet weight, I marvel at our bodies—
each other's bookmark—keeping alive the passage
called passion, the red quickening pulse that,
like the ratchet sound of a child's wind-up toy,
like the edge of the evaporating puddle,
fades only reluctantly as each cell whispers,
I am here. You are here. It matters.

World Enough

Whether I chalk it up to Newtonian physics
or just some impulse driven by the first whip
of a flagellating cell, I'm in it for the duration,
time and motion until the stop sign, and even then
the body's slow sinking into itself like fallen fruit.
I'm not talking about apples here—there is no moral—
only movement micro/macrocosmic, bodies mechanical
and protoplasmic, and how I watch the watch movement—
tick, tick—as if it's a tiny cosmic system, a study
in time and space—what else but continuum—because
God knows I want it quantifiable, a sort of
temporal hieroglyphic minute-to-minute record,
history of the path taken or not—tick, tick—my own
personal time bomb as we plunge through space and
each other, our bodies, if you believe quantum physics—
like the rest of the world—mostly made up of
space. In the midst of the falling, skydivers
aiming for a small plot of ground—"X" on the zoo map,
"G" in the woman's body, arrow pointing "You are here"—
I see it's a package deal, flesh and place—and
aren't we what we've always been—rhythm and matter
composed in treble and bass, songbird's trill
and Beethoven's da-da-da-DUM pressing into the shell
of the ear, a golden hum, cider sloshing
the sides of the jug. How I drink it in, a con
on death row looking for reprieve, the thub-dub behind
my bars quickening because, in this world of dung beetle
and rhinoplasty—tick, tick—it is all so wonderfully
with me I have to ask—who could willingly give it up?

Notes

Part One. Charles Simic states "A true confession: I believe in a soluble fish" in his essay "The Minotaur Loves His Labyrinth," from his collection of essays, *The Unemployed Fortune-Teller* (University of Michigan Press, 1994).

"Itch, Scratch." This poem is deeply indebted to Stephen Dunn's "From Nowhere" from *Local Visitations* (Norton, 2003).

"Memory." The Stevens poem cited is "The Emperor of Ice Cream" and the Dobyns poem is "The Party" from *Cemetery Nights* (Viking Penguin, 1987).

Part Two. Bertolt Brecht's "The Fishing Tackle" was translated by Lee Baxendall in *Bertolt Brecht: Poems 1913–1956* (Methuen, 1976).

"Of Snakes, Of Gluttony." The description of the anaconda is from Ben Belitt's translation of Neruda's "Some Beasts" in *Selected Poems of Pablo Neruda* (Grove Press, 1961). The Szymborska poem cited is "Pi" and appeared in *View with a Grain of Sand* (Harcourt Brace, 1995), translated by Stanislaw Baranczak and Clare Cavanaugh.

"Ladybug." Galway Kinnell's words are from his poem "Insomniac," which first appeared in *The New Yorker* on March 22, 2004.

Part Three. Jorie Graham's "Prayer" is the initial poem in her collection *Never* (HarperCollins, 2002).

"On Being Asked by a Student How You Know When a Poem Is Done." Andre Breton speaks of "a great chandelier of fish" in "Soluble Fish," *Manifestoes of Surrealism*, as translated by Richard Seaver and Helen R. Lane (University of Michigan Press, 1969). Dean Young coins the phrase "zpxtflo, unattainable zpxtflo" in "Blue Garden" from his collection *Skid* (University of Pittsburgh Press, 2002). Randall Jarrell's quote is from his essay "The Obscurity of the Poet" in *Poetry and the Age* (Random House, 1953). The complete statement is: "The poet writes his poem for its own sake, for the sake of that order of things in which the poem takes the place that has awaited it."

Other Books in the Crab Orchard Series in Poetry